Donald Trump's Triumph?
Short Analysis of his Positions
John Pierre Biddle Warden, ES.

1 TRUMP: Trump on Budget and the Economy

If debt reaches $24 T, that is the point of no return

If we have another 3 or 4 years--we are at $8 trillion now--we are soon going to be at $20 trillion. According to the economists--who I'm not big believers in, but, nevertheless, this is what they're saying--that $24 trillion--we're very close--that's the point of no return. $24 trillion. We will be there soon. That is when we become Greece. That is when we become a country that's unsalvageable. Moreover, we are going to be there very soon. We are going to be there very soon. [1]

1. Warden's comment:

---

[1] 2015 announcement speeches of 2016 presidential hopefuls,

Why does Mr. Trump choose to say we have another 3 or 4 years until we reach the point of no return, and we will end up with the country of Greece? Mr. Trump offers observations based on nothing more than a guess, and he offers no solution or solutions to the problem. So what he states is problematic in and of itself. If the number 24 trillion signifies the end of the world as we know it, why doesn't he have at least a prototype proposal for a solution to such a catastrophic problem? There is no explanation as to why the number 24 trillion is such an important number. The number 24 trillion means disaster then what is the solution to stop the United States from reaching that point? What then can we do to save the U.S. from becoming "unsalvageable" He offers at this stage no solution!

Along the same lines Mr. Trump states:

2. TRUMP **Prepare for upcoming crash, bigger than 1929**

I hope I am wrong, but I think we may be facing an economic crash like we've never seen before -probably sooner rather than later. The next president could be in office for a stock market crash worse than the one in 1929. I am not saying this crash will ruin us, but we have to anticipate it and know how to rebound. Right now I do not see the leadership we are going to need. [2]

2. **Warden's comment:**   Again there is an observation that says Mr. Trump thinks there will be an economic crash like we've never seen before. He says he is not saying it will ruin us, but again Mr. Trump offers no solution to a problem that may or may not happen. One would think that the American people deserve at least a prototype solution to such a catastrophe problem?

---

[2] The America We Deserve, by Donald Trump, p. 26, Jul 2, 2000

The questions Mr. Trump should be answering is what steps are necessary to avoid another economic crash? He has not listed the steps, nor the people he would hire to make sure that America does not enter another recession.

TRUMP 3: One-time 14.25% tax on wealth, to erase national debt

Trump wants to soak the rich, including himself. He proposed a 14.25% tax yesterday on the net worth of wealthy Americans.

He said the one-time tax package would: How would you guarantee that it is only a one-time tax package?

- Raise $5.7 trillion to erase the nation's debt and save $200 billion in annual interest payments

- Use the savings to save Social Security and slash taxes for the middle class

- Increase his personal tax bill by at least $725 million.

3. **Warden's comment:**   Who says that 5.7 trillion dollars will erase the nation's debt.   How will 200 billion be saved in annual interest payments? At the same time there is no explanation as to how that will exactly   save Social Security.   Nor how that particular figure will slash taxes for the middle class, or what percentage does that represent as a gain   for the   middle class? The figure sound like it was picked out of the sky with no real basis for that figure in reality.   How would that work? How did Mr. Trump arrive at the figure $725 million? Does that figure mean anything or is that a random figure.   Where are the details to prove that this approach will solve the Social Security problem and at the same time slash taxes on the middle class and ease the nation's debt? Isn't the question how do we stop the nation's debt and just not ease it? Isn't the question how do we make social security solvent? Isn't the question how much will

taxes be reduced on the middle class? Where is the mathematical proof for the whole scheme presented? Where is the solution to this approach? There is approach but no detailed follow through.

Donald Trump on Civil Rights

2000 Reform Primary Challenger for President

Disinvited from Red State gathering for misogynistic comments

Top presidential candidates took the stage this weekend at the Red State Gathering in Atlanta to discuss the future of the Republican Party. Each candidate and speaker are utilized their position to advance their vision for the future of the country and garner support from the public.

- "You could see there was blood coming out of her eyes, blood coming out of her wherever." -- Donald Trump, Republican presidential candidate, on Fox News host Megyn Kelly's performance as moderator for Thursday's GOP debate in Cleveland

- "I do not want Donald Trump in the room with my daughter tonight, so that is why he was disinvited." -- Erick Erickson, RedState Gathering organizer, after disinviting Donald Trump to the event. Trump was originally scheduled to speak at the RedState Tailgate near the College Football Hall of Fame[3]

Political correctness is country's problem, not my problem

---

[3] Atlanta Journal-Constitution on 2015 GOP RedState Gathering, Aug 8, 2015

Q: You do not use a politician's filter. However, that is not without its downsides, in particular, when it comes to women. You've called women you do not like "fat pigs, dogs, slobs, and disgusting animals."

TRUMP: Only Rosie O'Donnell!

Q: You once told a contestant on Celebrity Apprentice it would be a pretty picture to see her on her knees. Does that sound to you like the temperament of a man we should elect as president?

TRUMP: I think the big problem this country has been being politically correct. I do not have time for total political correctness. Moreover, to be honest with you, this country does not have time either. This country is in big trouble. We do not win anymore. We lose to China. We lose to Mexico both in trade and at the border. We lose to everybody. Moreover, frankly, what I say, and often it's fun, it is kidding. We have a good time. What I say is what I say. However, you know, we need strength, we need energy, we need quickness and we need a brain in this country to turn it around.[4]

Same-sex marriage is a state issue

What does Donald Trump believe? Social Issues: Marriage is between a man and a woman and should be defined a state by state.

---

[4] <u>Fox News/Facebook Top Ten First Tier debate transcript</u>, Aug 6, 2015

In a Bloomberg interview in January, the businessman asserted that he personally believes marriage is between a man and a woman. While he sees it as a state issue, Trump indicated that the Supreme Court could issue a ruling to determine the law.

Source: PBS News Hour "2016 Candidate Stands" series, Jun 16, 2015

No gay marriage; no same-sex partner benefits

On Thursday, Trump talked about "exploring" a presidential run, and was asked if he supports "allowing same-sex couples to marry."

Trump said "no," but didn't stop there. When asked whether gay couples should have access to "the same benefits as married couples," the mogul initially replied that his attitude on the issue was not yet "fully formed."

After thinking about it for a moment, however, Trump said: "As of this moment, I would say no and no" to gay marriage and civil benefits.

That answer may have resonated with Iowa conservatives who overwhelmingly opposed the Iowa Supreme Court's 2009 decision to overturn the state's gay marriage ban. But not in New York, home to one of the largest gay and lesbian communities in the US.

Trump was traveling Sunday and could not be reached for comment. Through a spokesman, he said only: "I am opposed to gay marriage." [5]

Tolerate diversity; prosecute hate crimes against gays

---

[5] New York Daily News, "Offends gay activist", Mar 7, 2011

One of our next president's most important goals must be to induce a greater tolerance for diversity. The senseless murder of Matthew Shepard in Wyoming-where, an innocent boy, was killed because of his sexual orientation- turned my stomach. We must work towards an America where these kinds of hate crimes are unthinkable. [6]

On Free Trade: We don't beat China or Japan or Mexico in trade

Our country is in serious trouble. We don't win anymore. We don't beat China in trade. We don't beat Japan, with their millions and millions of cars coming into this country, in trade. We can't beat Mexico, at the border or in trade.

---

[6] The America We Deserve, by Donald Trump, p. 31, Jul 2, 2000

We cannot do anything right. Our military has to be strengthened. Our vets have to be taken care of. We have to end Obama Care, and we have to make our country great again, and I will do that. [7]

Source: Fox News/Facebook Top Ten First Tier debate transcript Aug 6, 2015

On Government Reform: **I give to politicians; and they give back: that's broken!**

Q: You've donated to several Democratic candidates, Hillary Clinton included, Nancy Pelosi. You explained away those donations saying you did that to get business-related favors. And you said recently, quote, "When you give, they do whatever the hell you want them to do."

TRUMP: You had better believe it.

---

[7] Fox News/Facebook Top Ten First Tier debate transcript Aug 6, 2015

Q: So what specifically did they do?

TRUMP: If I ask them if I need them, you know, most of the people on this stage I've given to, so that you understand, much money. I will tell you that our system is broken. I gave to many people, before this, before two months ago, I was a business person. I give to everybody. When they call, I give. Moreover, do you know what? When I need something from them two years later, three years later, I call them, they are there for me. Moreover, that is a broken system.

Q: What did you get from Hillary Clinton?

TRUMP: Well, with Hillary Clinton, I said be at my wedding and she came to my wedding. You know why? She didn't have a choice because I gave to her foundation. [8]

On Health Care: The insurance companies have total control over politicians

Q: Obamacare is one of the things you call a disaster.

TRUMP: A complete disaster, yes.

Q: Saying it needs to be repealed & replaced.

TRUMP: Correct.

4. Warden's comment:

Again there is no indication as to what type of system you would replace from the Obama Care? Health care is still beyond the cost of most Americans. We use to make fun of the government spending $10,000 on toilet seats, and the Congress does nothing about- or Doctors charging $4000 on a case of conjunctivitis that would go away on its own without medical attention.

Q: Now, 15 years ago, you called yourself a liberal on health care. You were for a single-payer system, a Canadian-style system. Why you were for that then and why aren't you for it now?

TRUMP: As far as single payer, it works in Canada. It could have worked in a different age. What I'd like to see is a private system without the artificial lines around every state. I have a big company with thousands of employees. Moreover, if I'm negotiating in BY or NJ or CA, I have like one bidder. Nobody can bid. You know why? Because the insurance companies is making a fortune because they have control of the politicians. They are making a fortune. Get rid of the artificial lines and you will have yourself great plans. Moreover, then we have to take care of the people that can't take care of themselves. Moreover, I will do that through a different system.

Source: Fox News/Facebook Top Ten First Tier debate transcript Aug 6, 2015

On Immigration: We need wall on Mexican border, but ok to have a door in it

Q: You say that the Mexican government is sending criminals--rapists, drug dealers--across the frontier.

TRUMP: If it were not for me, you would not even be talking about illegal immigration. This was not a subject that was on anybody's mind until I brought it up at my announcement. The fact is, since then, many killings, murders, crime, drugs are pouring across the border, our money going out and the drugs coming in. Moreover, I said we need to build a wall, and it has to be built quickly. Moreover, I do not mind having a beautiful big door in that wall so that people can come into this country legally. However, we need to build a wall, we need to keep illegals out. [9]

On Immigration: **Mexican government is sending criminals across the border**

[9] Fox News/Facebook Top Ten First Tier debate transcript Aug 6, 2015.

Q: You have repeatedly said that you have evidence that the Mexican government is sending criminals across the border, but you have refused or declined to share it. Could you share your proof?

TRUMP: Border Patrol people that I talk to, they say this is what's happening. Because our leaders are stupid. Moreover, the Mexican government is much smarter, much sharper, and much more cunning. Moreover, they send the bad ones over because they do not want to pay for them. They do not want to take care of them. Why should they when the stupid leaders of the United States will do it for them? Moreover, that is what is happening whether you like it or not. [10]

---

[10] Fox News/Facebook Top Ten First Tier debate transcript Aug 6, 2015.

5. Warden's comments: Mr. Trump states that he will build a wall and it will be easy and built fast. However, he does not go into detail as to exactly how he would protect the American people from illegal drugs and terrorist that are filtering into our country from all borders. A wall is fine but only as a beginning step. How do you guarantee no landings on the Gulf of Mexico, on the Atlantic and Pacific Oceans and the Canadian border? None of these avenues of possible terrorist infiltration is addressed by any of the candidates. No one dreams large anymore. How about not only a wall but a deep canal similar to the Panama Canal that would address trying to tunnel under the wall and would eventually lead to cheaper goods for the American people in the long run, would furnish private companies with challenges to build, and ensure a large a working labor force for about a century to build on both our southern and northern borders. The Saint Lawrence Sea Way already exists along with the Great Lakes so part of that proposed sea canal already exists. The Gulf of

Mexico exists so part of the proposed southern seaway already exists. This is a possible way to improve the economic lives of the American people, increase revenues from trade, and dream to build. Also the canal would be flooded with sea water and America could begin building desalination plants on the new sea canals to furnish the interior with fresh water in times of drought. America needs to dream big. They said we could not build the Panama Canal but we did. As President you could issue temporary executive orders on immigration until the Congress acts on the problem.

On Principles & Values: I want to win as a Republican, but might run as Independent

Q: Is there anyone on stage which is unwilling tonight to pledge your support to the eventual nominee of the Republican Party and pledge to not run an independent campaign against that person. [Only Trump raises hand]. Mr. Trump to be clear, you are standing on a Republican primary debate stage.

TRUMP: I fully understand.

Q: And that experts say an independent run would almost certainly hand the race over to Democrats & likely another Clinton. You cannot say tonight that you can make that pledge?

TRUMP: I cannot say. I have to respect the person that [is nominated], if it's not me, I can totally make that pledge. If I am the nominee, I will pledge I will not run as an independent. We want to win; I want to win as the Republican; I want to run as the Republican nominee.

RAND PAUL: He's already hedging his bet. Maybe he supports Clinton, or maybe he runs as an independent. [11]

Q: You're not going to make the pledge tonight?

TRUMP: I will not make the pledge at this time.

6. Warden's comment: None. It is not a real issue in a democracy.

On Principles & Values: In NYC almost everyone is Democrat, but I'm Republican

Q: In 2004, you said in most cases you identified as a Democrat. When did you actually become a Republican?

[11] Fox News/Facebook Top Ten First Tier debate transcript Aug 6, 2015

TRUMP: I come from a place, New York City, which is virtual, I mean, it is almost exclusively Democrat. And I have really started to see some of the negatives--as an example, and I have a lot of liking for [Jeb Bush], but the last number of months of his brother's administration were a catastrophe. Moreover, unfortunately, those few months gave us President Obama. Moreover, you cannot be happy about that.

On War & Peace: Opposed Iraq war in 2004 & predicted Mideast destabilization

In July of 2004, I came out strongly against the war with Iraq, because it was going to destabilize the Middle East. Moreover, I am the only one on this stage that knew that and had the vision to say it. Moreover, that is exactly what happened. Moreover, the Middle East became totally destabilized. [12]

---

[12] Fox News/Facebook Top Ten First Tier debate transcript Aug 6, 2015

On War & Peace: Disgraceful deal gives Iran a lot & gets nothing for us

Q: On Obama's Iranian nuclear deal?

TRUMP: I would be so different from what you have right now. Like, the polar opposite. We have a president who does not have a clue. I would say he is incompetent, but I do not want to do that because that's not nice. But if you look at the deals we make, whether it's the nuclear deal with 24 hour periods--and by the way, before you get to the 24 hours, you have to go through a system. You look at Sgt. Bergdahl, we get Bergdahl, a traitor, and they get 5 of the big, great killer leaders that they want. We have people in Washington that don't know what they are doing. Now, with Iran, we are making a deal, you would say, we want out our prisoners. We want all these things, and we do not get anything. We are giving them $150 billion dollars plus. I'll tell you what, if Iran were a stock, you folks should go out and buy it right now because you'll quadruple--this, what's happening in Iran, is a disgrace, and it's going to lead to destruction in large portions of the world [13]

13

7. Warden's comment:

Yes you came out against the war in the Middle East in 2004 because you said it would destabilized the Middle East. The Middle East was already destabilized and it has continued to be destabilized but not so much because of the war but because now and in the past some ugly forces have raised their heads and continue one of the oldest strategies in the world- divide and conquer. In Syria we see a dictator that is using the situation to divide his own people so that he can conquer to remain in power. Israel and Palestine are still questions that aid in the destabilization of the Middle East. The previous Iran-Iraq war was also a factor in destabilizing the Middle East. So the area was already destabilized.

In Iran we see a Nation lead by a factional renegade religion that has for forty years called America the Great Satan. Iraq was torn apart not only by the war waged by the United States but it is still torn apart by issues of religion that cannot see a way to reconcile their differences peaceably. You could have offered a prototype solution such as: Iran is part of the key to the solution in the Middle East and such an irresponsible nation should never have privy to nuclear secrets.

If they want to use nuclear power for domestic power is one thing but the United States; the whole world needs assurances that nuclear power is used in a peaceful manner. To do otherwise is to arm the enemy with the power of massive destruction and say go ahead and shoot. It is complete nuclear suicide to trust and not verify. You could have suggested as a prototype solution a 100% embargo of Iran by our Navy and Airforce by executive order. Then you can negotiate from a position of strength rather than weakness. We should get the countries that border Iran to join in that embargo and see that nothing goes in or out of Iran on pain of the use of our military weapons. Then if Iran wants to negotiate on the basis of verification then the embargo parts would be lifted in stages as the Congress feels secure to do so. On the other hand, if it is true that scientist can tell how long it has taken to clean up nuclear sites because of the nature of nuclear material, and scientist can prove that statement then a deal with Iran might go forward. It has been stated by a noted scientist that inspection of sites is not like dumping drugs down the toilet. You can tell what material they are using even after a long while so there would be no cover up. However, the very serious question still remains how do scientist tell whether in a nuclear cleanup to hide things—how can them tell whether the material is to be used for peace or war? What nuclear element would only be used in war? Again the reporters have failed to conduct any in-depth coverage of the candidates and the debates are superficial and meaningless so far.

While there is a recognizable phenomenon of vast crowds showing up at the debates and presentation by Mr. Trump across the nation, I fear it is more because of his celebrity status than his substance as a politician. I wish Mr. Trump well in his endeavors but yearn for more prototype solutions to America's problems. Only the people will choose who will be their next leader.

www.ingramcontent.com/pod-product-compliance
Lightning Source LLC
Chambersburg PA
CBHW042239290526
45792CB00021B/825